MW00427388

DAILY ACTS OF
KINDNESS

A JOURNAL TO INSPIRE CONNECTION AND JOY

WRITTEN BY MARY MCGLONE

PETER PAUPER PRESS, INC.
WHITE PLAINS, NEW YORK

WITH GRATITUDE FOR ALL THE KIND PEOPLE IN MY LIFE

AND FOR MY DAUGHTER, CLARE, WHO DANCES IN MY HEART

PETER PAUPER PRESS
Fine Books and Gifts Since 1928

OUR COMPANY

In 1928, at the age of twenty-two, Peter Beilenson began printing books on a small press in the basement of his parents' home in Larchmont, New York. Peter—and later, his wife, Edna—sought to create fine books that sold at "prices even a pauper could afford."

Today, still family owned and operated, Peter Pauper Press continues to honor our founders' legacy—and our customers' expectations—of beauty, quality, and value.

Cover designed by Heather Zschock
Interior designed by Margaret Rubiano

Images used under license from Shutterstock.com

Copyright © 2020
Peter Pauper Press, Inc.
202 Mamaroneck Avenue
White Plains, NY 10601 USA
All rights reserved
ISBN 978-1-4413-3287-5
Printed in China
7 6 5 4 3 2 1

Visit us at www.peterpauper.com

INTRODUCTION

It's easy to focus on the negativity in our lives. But have you noticed how even one small, unexpected gesture can turn your whole day around?

Three days after beginning this book, I broke my right wrist (yes, I'm right-handed). Then the unexpected kindnesses rolled in: offers to type, advice on dictation programs, meals dropped off at dinnertime. Every day, my dishes were washed and my garden was watered. I knew this book would get written. It was a gift to live kindness while I wrote it.

This book is about kindness: noticing it, enjoying it, spreading it. Each page invites playful reflection on what kindness, community, and joy mean to you.

This book is an *invitation*—to be kind, yes, but also to play and to find your joy, to treat yourself with kindness, and to live more fully in the world. Enjoy your journey!

RECALL AN UNEXPECTED KINDNESS SOMEONE DID FOR YOU, RECENTLY OR IN THE DISTANT PAST.

Who did it?

When?

What was the kindness?

What about it touched you?

No act of kindness,
no matter
how small,
is ever wasted.

—AESOP

Kindness Day

TODAY, LOOK FOR AN OPPORTUNITY TO DO AN ACT OF KINDNESS, LARGE OR SMALL.

My kind act:

How did I feel?

CIRCLE THE WORDS AND PHRASES YOU ASSOCIATE WITH
KINDNESS, THINKING ABOUT BOTH ITS POSITIVE AND
CHALLENGING ASPECTS:

STRENGTH

time

effort

risk

BEING PRESENT

polite

listening

AWARENESS

HUMOR

intrusive

vulnerability

bravery

COMMUNITY

pushover

COURAGE

courtesy

draining

forgiveness

generosity

NOTICING

growth

INSIGHT

inconvenient

RESPONDING
TO NEED

Childlike Joy

RECONNECT WITH YOUR INNER CHILD.

BLOW BUBBLES

READ A PICTURE BOOK

CATCH FIREFLIES AT DUSK

RUN AND JUMP

HULA HOOP

PLAY TIDDLY WINKS

This is how I played today:

_To play is to live
life to its fullest._

— ELISABETH KÜBLER-ROSS

THOUSANDS OF CANDLES CAN BE LIGHTED FROM
A SINGLE CANDLE, AND THE LIFE OF THE CANDLE
WILL NOT BE SHORTENED. HAPPINESS NEVER
DECREASES BY BEING SHARED.

- THE TEACHING OF BUDDHA

What brings you joy that you can share with somebody else?

Who can you share it with?

How can you share it?

If/when you share your joy: How did it go?

WRITE AN **ACROSTIC POEM** ABOUT KINDNESS. THAT'S A POEM WHERE THE FIRST LETTER OF EACH WORD SPELLS OUT ANOTHER WORD OR PHRASE WHEN READ FROM TOP TO BOTTOM. FOR EXAMPLE:

FULFILLMENT

RECIPROCITY

INSPIRING

EXCELLENT

NOURISH

**DOUBLE THE JOY,
HALF THE SORROW**

Each line can be a kind act, a person, an opportunity, or a word you associate with kindness.

K
I
N
D
N
E
S
S

A journey of a thousand miles begins with a single step.

—LAO TZU

Start Small

REACH BEYOND YOUR DAILY ROUTINE WITH A **SMALL, SIMPLE KINDNESS** TODAY. HERE ARE SOME IDEAS:

- Feed the birds.
- Donate food to a food pantry.
- Call an elderly relative or neighbor.
- Let a car or pedestrian ahead of you in line.
- Give someone (anyone!) a compliment.
- Send a card (any occasion, no occasion!) to someone.
- _____

Circle the one you did, or add your own!

How did it go?

IN A WORLD WHERE YOU CAN BE ANYTHING, BE KIND.

NO MATTER WHO YOU ARE, WHAT YOU DO, WHATEVER YOUR STATION IN LIFE OR INNER STRUGGLES, YOU HAVE THE POWER TO BE KIND. THROUGH MANY TRANSITIONS IN LIFE, KINDNESS CAN BE A CONSTANT PART OF **WHO YOU ARE**.

Reflect on this: Is kindness part of who you are? Do you want it to be?

How can you make it part of everything you do?

ONE OUGHT, EVERY DAY AT LEAST, TO HEAR A LITTLE SONG, READ A GOOD POEM, SEE A FINE PICTURE AND, IF POSSIBLE, SPEAK A FEW REASONABLE WORDS.

— JOHANN WOLFGANG VON GOETHE

So today . . . read a poem or hear a song!

Doodle as you listen to or contemplate the music of the words.

What poem or song did you enjoy?

Title:

Artist or poet:

What lines resonated with you?

What about them struck you?

Color this in with your favorite markers or colored pencils:

SOW KINDNESS
REAP BEAUTY

WE CAN BE PATIENT AND STAND IN OUR POWER AT THE SAME TIME.

— ELISABETH KÜBLER-ROSS

PATIENCE AND KINDNESS DO NOT MEAN BEING TAKEN ADVANTAGE OF. SOMETIMES THE STRONGEST WAY TO ACHIEVE A GOAL IS TO STATE YOUR INTENTION AND STAND IN PATIENCE. **QUIET POWER** IS VERY EFFECTIVE.

What are some situations in which you could stand compassionate but firm in your power?

_____

_____

_____

_____

_____

If you try it: How did it go?

WITHOUT COURAGE...
WE CAN'T BE KIND, TRUE,
MERCIFUL, GENEROUS,
OR HONEST.

—MAYA ANGELOU

What does courage mean to you?

What's one courageous act that you feel good about having done?

Where in your life could you be braver?

KIND = BRAVE

BE BRAVE. BE KIND. (BE KIND OF BRAVE?)

Being kind is a courageous act.

We think it's "none of our business" when a parent is struggling to soothe a toddler having a temper tantrum in the supermarket, a pedestrian is trying to cross the street, or a stranger is crying on a park bench. But when everyone else is walking by, it takes courage to care.

THIS IS BRAVE KINDNESS.

Look for a kindness opportunity that requires you to be a little brave, and seize that opportunity.

What brave kindness did you do?

How did it go?

PRACTICE KIND NONJUDGMENT AND LOVING ACCEPTANCE.

NEXT TIME YOU FIND YOURSELF ANGRY AT SOMEONE'S ACTIONS
(A CAR CUTS AHEAD OF YOU, SOMEONE IS RUDE) ... PAUSE.

REMIND YOURSELF THAT YOU DON'T KNOW WHAT'S HAPPENING
IN THE PERSON'S LIFE. GIVE THEM THE BENEFIT OF THE DOUBT.
BREATHE AND ... BE KIND.

What are some things strangers do that drive you crazy?

What are some kind ways you could react, or refrain from reacting, instead of getting mad?

Be kind to unkind people.
They need it the most.

— ASHLEIGH BRILLIANT

 # JOY COLLAGE

ON THESE PAGES, PASTE WORDS AND IMAGES THAT BRING YOU JOY. CLIP THEM FROM MAGAZINES, NEWSPAPERS, AND OTHER PRINTED MATERIALS, OR PRINT THEM OUT YOURSELF.

NURTURE JOY

VENTURE OUTSIDE AND EXPLORE YOUR NEIGHBORHOOD OR A PARK. NOTICE BEAUTY. TRY TO USE ALL YOUR SENSES. SOME THINGS YOU MIGHT NOTICE:

- The way sunlight filters through leaves
- The unexpected color of a house or building
- The sound of laughter or voices in conversation
- The shapes formed by ice or snow on the ground
- The smell of plants, or of food cooking
- The feeling in the air just before it rains

Where did you go?

What did you notice?

THE UNIVERSE IS
FULL OF
MAGICAL THINGS
PATIENTLY
WAITING FOR
OUR WITS TO
GROW SHARPER.

— EDEN PHILLPOTTS

LOOK AROUND YOUR LIVING SPACE WITH NEW EYES. SEEK OUT
SOMETHING BEAUTIFUL, INTERESTING, OR FUNNY IN YOUR HOME
THAT YOU SEE OFTEN BUT HAVEN'T TAKEN NOTE OF IN A WHILE. IT
COULD BE THE SUN COMING IN THROUGH YOUR WINDOW, A PIECE OF
ART, A FAVORITE BOOK, OR A JOKE GIFT FROM A FRIEND.

What did you find?

What about it do you enjoy?

DO YOUR LITTLE BIT
OF GOOD WHERE YOU ARE;
IT'S THOSE LITTLE BITS OF
GOOD PUT TOGETHER THAT
OVERWHELM
THE WORLD.

— DESMOND TUTU

YOU **KNOW** THOSE PEOPLE YOU "**OWE**" A PHONE CALL OR
MESSAGE TO? (COME ON, WE *ALL* HAVE THEM!)

YOU MISS THEM, IT'S BEEN A WHILE, YOU REALLY SHOULD CALL . . .
IF ONLY YOU HAD (MADE) THE TIME . . .

Write their names below. Beginning today, contact one person. Send
a text, an email, a postcard, or call (and, yes, it counts if you leave a
voicemail). Write the date you contacted each person. Then give yourself
a star. Color the star any color you want.

WRITE THEIR NAMES HERE: **DATE:**

today!   ☆

☆

☆

☆

☆

☆

☆

☆

☆

☆

There! Doesn't that feel good?

BE KIND TO YOURSELF. CIRCLE THE THINGS THAT SOUND GOOD TO YOU RIGHT NOW:

TAKE A NAP

take a walk

stretch

wear a favorite
article of clothing

SLOW DOWN

eat something nourishing

TAKE A BATH

GIVE YOURSELF A
COMPLIMENT
WHEN YOU LOOK IN
THE MIRROR

get some exercise

READ OR WATCH SOMETHING FUN

PICK AT LEAST ONE, AND SET ASIDE A MOMENT TO DO IT.

What kindness can you show yourself today?

How do you feel afterward?

Is this something you might want to do more often?

SOMETIMES YOUR JOY IS THE SOURCE
OF YOUR SMILE, BUT SOMETIMES
YOUR SMILE CAN BE THE
SOURCE OF YOUR JOY.

—THICH NHAT HANH

Kindness Day

TODAY, LOOK FOR AN OPPORTUNITY TO DO AN ACT OF KINDNESS, LARGE OR SMALL.

My kind act:

How did I feel?

If you are kind,
people may accuse
you of selfish, ulterior
motives; be kind
anyway.

The good you do
today, people will often
forget tomorrow;
do good anyway.

—MOTHER TERESA

DOING GOOD IS NOT ABOUT BEING APPRECIATED; IT'S ABOUT HOW IT CHANGES YOU.

DO A FAVOR FOR SOMEONE YOU CARE ABOUT TODAY, WHETHER IT IS NOTICED OR NOT, AND BE AWARE OF HOW YOU FEEL.

What I did:

How I felt:

REMEMBER SEVENTH GRADE?

ADOLESCENCE CAN BE A DIFFICULT, LONELY TIME, AND A LITTLE KINDNESS CAN GO A LONG WAY. WRITE A **LETTER OF ENCOURAGEMENT** TO YOUR SEVENTH-GRADE SELF, FULL OF ALL THE THINGS YOU WISH SOMEONE HAD TOLD YOU.

Dear _____,

With good wishes,
Your grown-up self

PRAISE THE YOUNG
AND THEY
WILL BLOSSOM.

— IRISH PROVERB

EVERYONE HAS **OBSTACLES TO KINDNESS**: THINGS THAT MAKE IT HARDER FOR THEM TO BE KIND. BELOW ARE SOME COMMON ONES, AND SOME WAYS YOU CAN BEGIN TO ADDRESS THEM, IF THEY APPLY TO YOU. (THESE THINGS AREN'T SOLUTIONS, OF COURSE— THEY'RE JUST SIMPLE STEPS YOU CAN TAKE RIGHT AWAY.)

OBSTACLES TO KINDNESS	WHAT I CAN DO
I am busy and distracted.	Practice redirecting your thoughts away from your plans and to-do list, and toward whatever you're experiencing right now, in the moment.
My stress level makes it hard to focus on anything else.	Look for ways you can reach out and ask for a little help.
I am in my own head all the time.	Make eye contact with and smile at one person.
I am shy. It's hard for me to speak to people I don't know.	Look for a thing you can compliment—someone's rock concert T-shirt, a book in someone's hand that you read and liked—and tell them you think it's cool.
I mind my own business.	Find a way to engage with your community, whether it's volunteering or saying hi to your neighbors, and see what results.
I just don't notice. I must have blinders on.	Whenever you have a spare moment, practice deliberately directing your attention toward the world around you. It gets more intuitive with repetition.
I am always looking down at my phone.	Turn your phone off for one hour today.

WRITE IN SOME OF YOUR OWN PERSONAL OBSTACLES TO KINDNESS, AND IDEAS FOR ADDRESSING THEM:

OBSTACLES TO KINDNESS	WHAT I CAN DO

Commit to one thing today.

Today I will _____

to help me on the road to kindness.

You can always, always give something,
even if it is only kindness! —ANNE FRANK

WHAT IS A TALENT OF YOURS THAT COULD BE USED TO MAKE OTHER PEOPLE HAPPIER, SAFER, OR MORE COMFORTABLE? (A SKILL? A TYPE OF STRENGTH? KNOWLEDGE OR INSIGHT? SOMETHING THAT'S EASIER FOR YOU THAN IT IS FOR MOST PEOPLE?)

How could you use it to help someone?

Who could you use it to help?

The mountains are calling, and I must go.

—JOHN MUIR

WHAT PLACES MAKE YOU HAPPY? LIST LOCAL AND FARAWAY
SPOTS ALIKE.

Pick a nearby spot, and make plans to go there with a friend, family
member, or acquaintance soon.
Where are you going, when, and with whom?

SAY

Thank You

TO SOMEONE.

THOSE ARE BEAUTIFUL WORDS WE ALL LIKE TO HEAR.

MAYBE SOMEONE SPOKE UP FOR YOU WHEN YOU NEEDED IT, OR GAVE YOU EMOTIONAL SUPPORT AT A VULNERABLE TIME, OR INSPIRED YOU WHEN YOU FELT ALONE.

THE MORE TIME HAS PASSED, THE BETTER— IT WILL MEAN EVEN MORE!

Person:

Thank you for:

How you will thank them (in person, phone call, card):

After you thank them: What was their response?

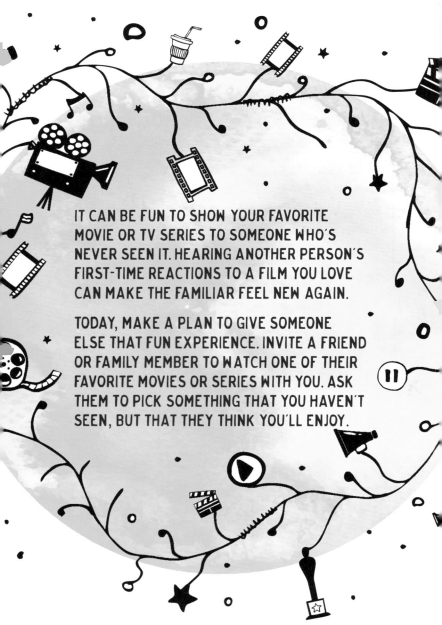

IT CAN BE FUN TO SHOW YOUR FAVORITE MOVIE OR TV SERIES TO SOMEONE WHO'S NEVER SEEN IT. HEARING ANOTHER PERSON'S FIRST-TIME REACTIONS TO A FILM YOU LOVE CAN MAKE THE FAMILIAR FEEL NEW AGAIN.

TODAY, MAKE A PLAN TO GIVE SOMEONE ELSE THAT FUN EXPERIENCE. INVITE A FRIEND OR FAMILY MEMBER TO WATCH ONE OF THEIR FAVORITE MOVIES OR SERIES WITH YOU. ASK THEM TO PICK SOMETHING THAT YOU HAVEN'T SEEN, BUT THAT THEY THINK YOU'LL ENJOY.

Who are you watching with, and when?

_____

What are you watching?

_____

When you watch, be sure to tell the person who showed you the movie or TV series at least one thing you liked about it.

What did you like?

_____

_____

_____

_____

Now you and this person have another thing to talk about!

OUR WINGS ARE SMALL BUT
THE RIPPLES OF THE HEART
ARE INFINITE.

—AMIT RAY

KINDNESS DAY

TODAY, LOOK FOR AN OPPORTUNITY TO DO AN ACT OF KINDNESS, LARGE OR SMALL.

My kind act:

How did I feel?

Won't you be
my neighbor?

—FRED ROGERS

THE WORLD CAN FEEL LIKE A BIG, LONELY PLACE—BUT WE HAVE
THE POWER TO CREATE COMMUNITY AND CONNECT TO OTHER
PEOPLE. SOME WAYS TO CREATE COMMUNITY IN YOUR HOME,
WORKPLACE, OR TOWN:

- Go to a high school play or concert.
- Join a community garden.
- Go to a local park and pet a dog.
- Bring jigsaw puzzles to a nearby senior center.
- Attend an event at your local library.
- Read a book, garden, or work on a project in your front yard.
  Say hello to whoever passes by.

Add your own ideas:

CIRCLE ONE YOU CAN DO THIS WEEK.

laugh!

TROUBLE KNOCKED AT THE DOOR, BUT, HEARING LAUGHTER, HURRIED AWAY.

—BENJAMIN FRANKLIN

What always makes you laugh?

TRUE KINSHIP TAKES
A WARM HEART. IN ESSENCE,
IT IS ABOUT BEING TOGETHER,
DEEPLY HONESTLY.

—ILSE CRAWFORD

Kindred Spirits

PERHAPS WHEN WE SHARE KINDNESS WE BECOME KIN.

Who are your "kin" (people you feel connected to)?

Reach out to one of these people today, and say hi.

The act of forgiveness
takes place in our
own mind.

—LOUISE HAY

IT HAS BEEN SAID THAT **FORGIVENESS** DOES MORE TO HEAL THE PERSON WHO WAS HURT THAN THE PERSON WHO INFLICTED THE HURT. THINK OF ONE PERSON WHO HAS WRONGED YOU. FORGIVE THEM, WHETHER THEY HAVE ASKED FOR IT OR NOT.

FILL THIS IN:

_____ (name),

I choose to forgive you for _____.

It is time to be liberated from holding a grudge or feeling bad.

I imagine a future in which you and I are _____

(peaceful, friendly, separate).

Thank you for helping me to grow in kindness.

Signed, _____

You don't need to send this message to the person. This forgiveness is for you.

TRUE FORGIVENESS IS WHEN YOU CAN SAY, "THANK YOU FOR THAT EXPERIENCE."

—OPRAH WINFREY

IF YOU HAD TO PICK ONE, WHAT IS YOUR *best quality?*

Have you shared it recently? If not, with whom could you share it, and how?

DRAW SOMETHING THAT REPRESENTS THAT QUALITY HERE:

Make
something!

MAKE . . .

AMENDS

it up to someone

dinner

A DATE

FRIENDS

an impression

CIRCLE ONE, AND PLAN OUT HOW YOU'LL DO IT:

IF YOU WANT TO GO FAST, GO ALONE.

IF YOU WANT TO GO FAR, GO TOGETHER.

WE TEND TO DO THINGS INDEPENDENTLY AND IN ISOLATION. THIS IS IMPORTANT FOR SOME TASKS, BUT SOMETIMES **WORKING WITH OTHERS** COULD MAKE EVERYONE'S ROAD EASIER.

DO YOU HAVE A PROJECT OR GOAL THAT YOU COULD INCLUDE SOMEONE ELSE IN?

Goal:

....

....

Who might help:

....

....

....

How you could tackle this as a team:

....

....

....

....

....

....

....

....

....

....

LIFE APPEARS TO ME
TOO SHORT TO BE SPENT IN
NURSING ANIMOSITY OR
REGISTERING WRONGS.

—CHARLOTTE BRONTË

EVEN WHEN OTHERS ARE RUDE, WE CAN MEET THAT RUDENESS
WITH KINDNESS. IT MAY SURPRISE THEM, AND WE WILL MAINTAIN
OUR PEACE OF MIND.

HOW CAN YOU RESPOND THE NEXT TIME SOMEONE IS RUDE TO
YOU?

When we give cheerfully
and accept gratefully,
everyone is blessed.

—MAYA ANGELOU

NAME SOMEONE IN YOUR LIFE WHOM YOU DEEPLY APPRECIATE, AND HAVEN'T EXPRESSED YOUR APPRECIATION TO IN A WHILE:

What can you say or do to make this person feel appreciated?

WRITE A NOTE TO YOURSELF, EXPRESSING WHAT YOU MOST ADMIRE AND VALUE ABOUT YOU.

Dear _____ ,
　　　　　　　　　　　　(name)

You are a _____
　　　　　　　　(wonderful, special, amazing)

person. You aren't perfect (no one is), but that isn't the goal anyway.

You are a _____ and
　　　　　　　　(sincere, caring)

_____ person. You have
(generous, compassionate, kindhearted)

a special gift of _____ .
　　　　　(humor, noticing, gentleness, honesty, integrity)

You have the ability to make other people's lives better. Two

people whose lives are better because of you are:

_____ and

_____.

Don't forget how much you matter. Keep being your

_____ self.

(awesome, amazing, wonderful)

_____,

(Fondly, Love, Always)

an admirer

READ IT THE NEXT TIME YOU ARE HAVING A HARD DAY.

What small, easy thing can you do today to bring yourself joy?

....

....

....

....

When can you do it?

....

....

What about this brings you joy?

....

....

....

....

....

....

....

....

....

The Ripple Effect

DID YOU EVER NOTICE THAT KINDNESS IS CONTAGIOUS? YOU LET ANOTHER CAR AHEAD OF YOU IN TRAFFIC AND AT THE NEXT INTERSECTION, THEY LET SOMEONE ELSE IN; YOU CHAT WITH SOMEONE IN LINE AT A STORE AND THEN THE CASHIER CHATS WITH YOU.

- Think of a kindness someone did for you that enabled you to do a kindness for someone else. It can be small or large.

- On the next page, write the kindness you received in the center ripple.

- Write the kindness you did as a result in the next ripple.

- Do you know if the person you were kind to was kind to someone else in turn? If not, write something they could have done. That's the third ripple.

KINDNESS CREATES POSSIBILITY. WHO KNOWS WHAT YOUR KINDNESS CAN MAKE POSSIBLE, A FEW MORE RIPPLES OUT?

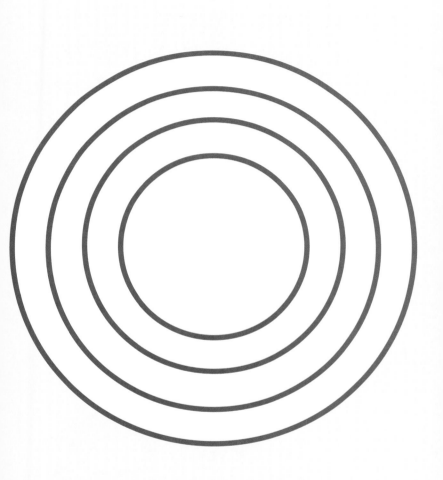

THREE THINGS IN HUMAN LIFE ARE
IMPORTANT. THE FIRST IS TO BE
KIND. THE SECOND IS TO BE KIND.
AND THE THIRD IS TO BE KIND.

—HENRY JAMES

TAKE PHOTOS OF FIVE BEAUTIFUL THINGS TODAY. SHARE ONE WITH A FRIEND.

What did you photograph?

1
2
3
4
5

Who did you share it with?

Shall we make a new rule of life
from tonight: always to try to be
a little kinder than is necessary?

—J.M. BARRIE

Kindness Day

Today, look for an opportunity to do an act of kindness, large or small.

My kind act:

_____

_____

_____

_____

How did I feel?

_____

_____

_____

_____

"I DON'T FEEL VERY MUCH LIKE
POOH TODAY," SAID POOH.
"THERE, THERE," SAID PIGLET. "I'LL BRING
YOU TEA AND HONEY UNTIL YOU DO."

— A. A. MILNE, *WINNIE-THE-POOH*

SOMETIMES WHAT HELPS MOST IS **VERY SIMPLE**.

BE PIGLET FOR SOMEBODY: INSTEAD OF JUDGING OR SOLVING, SIMPLY OFFER THE COMFORT OF YOUR PRESENCE.

Today I will take care of:

What will you do?

Receiving Kindness

WE BUILD COMMUNITY BY BOTH GIVING AND RECEIVING.

IT IS DIFFICULT FOR MANY OF US TO RECEIVE KINDNESS, THOUGH WE GIVE IT.

WHY?

DO YOU THINK YOU DON'T DESERVE IT? (WE ALL DESERVE TO BE TREATED KINDLY.)

DO YOU FEEL OBLIGATED TO SOMEONE IF THEY HELP YOU?

IS THAT HOW YOU VIEW IT WHEN YOU ARE THE ONE GIVING KINDNESS?

When do you have trouble receiving kind words or actions?

What do you think makes it hard for you to receive kindness?

IT IS OUR SPIRITUAL
RESPONSIBILITY TO RECEIVE.

KINDNESS EXPECTS NOTHING
IN RETURN.

Say Yes!

ISN'T THAT A BEAUTIFUL WORD?

What can you say "yes!" to today?

Let us be kind to one another,
for most of us are
fighting a hard battle.

—IAN MACLAREN

What is a judgment other people make about you that isn't accurate?

What are some judgments you've recently made about other people?

Is it possible that your judgments aren't accurate?

TODAY, TRY TO WITHHOLD JUDGMENT.

SHARE EVERYTHING.
PLAY FAIR.
DON'T HIT PEOPLE.
PUT THINGS BACK WHERE
YOU FOUND THEM.
CLEAN UP YOUR OWN MESS.
DON'T TAKE THINGS THAT AREN'T YOURS.
SAY YOU'RE SORRY WHEN
YOU HURT SOMEBODY.

— ROBERT FULGHUM, *ALL I REALLY NEED
TO KNOW I LEARNED IN KINDERGARTEN*

Are there any lessons here that you are still working on?

Patience is a conquering virtue.

— GEOFFREY CHAUCER

WHO IS SOMEONE YOU STRUGGLE WITH BEING KIND TOWARD?

List their good qualities here.

1.

2.

(Okay, maybe you can only think of one! ☺)

KEEP THIS IN MIND NEXT TIME YOU SEE THE PERSON.

AT WHAT TIME OF DAY IS YOUR ENERGY LOWEST? DRAW THE HANDS ON THE CLOCK.

SET AN ALARM FOR THAT TIME, AND WHEN IT GOES OFF, TAKE A
BREAK FROM YOUR ROUTINE TO DO SOMETHING KIND.

GIVE A COMPLIMENT

bring someone
a cup of coffee

post a corny
cartoon on the
refrigerator

SEND A
CHEERFUL EMAIL
TO A FRIEND

You cannot do a
kindness too soon.

— RALPH WALDO EMERSON

AS FAR AS POSSIBLE WITHOUT SURRENDER BE ON GOOD TERMS WITH ALL PERSONS.

— MAX EHRMANN, *DESIDERATA*

IT IS GOOD TO GET ALONG WITH EVERYONE—BUT ONLY IF YOU DON'T COMPROMISE WHO YOU ARE, AND YOUR **PRINCIPLES**. STANDING FOR YOUR VALUES, AND STANDING UP FOR OTHER PEOPLE WHEN NECESSARY, IS A STRONG ACT OF KINDNESS.

What are some principles you will not compromise?

1.

2.

3.

4.

5.

6.

7.

8.

9.

10.

Start your day with kindness.

WHAT CAN YOU DO BEFORE YOU EVEN GET OUT OF BED IN THE MORNING THAT IS KIND—TO YOURSELF OR SOMEONE ELSE? (THINK: BREATHE DEEPLY, KISS THE PERSON NEXT TO YOU, SLEEP FOR FIVE MORE MINUTES.)

DON'T BE BREAKING
YOUR SHIN ON
A STOOL THAT'S
NOT IN YOUR WAY.

— IRISH PROVERB

What is one thing in your life that is causing you stress?

And here's the important question:

Do you need to *do anything* about it? If so, what?

Is it possible that your focus on it is giving it more power than it deserves?

MANY PROBLEMS FADE WITH TIME.
WALK AROUND THE STOOL.

DON'T WORRY ABOUT WHAT HAPPENS ONCE YOU CREATE AN ACT OF KINDNESS.

HOW IT IS RECEIVED IS OUT OF YOUR HANDS. ALL THAT MATTERS IS WHAT YOU DO.

Today I will . . .

_____

_____

_____

. . . and not be concerned about the result.

DON'T JUDGE EACH DAY BY THE HARVEST YOU REAP BUT BY THE SEEDS THAT YOU PLANT.

— ROBERT LOUIS STEVENSON

I can live for two months on a good compliment.

— MARK TWAIN

What is the best compliment you've ever received? (I bet it wasn't about your shoes!)

_____

_____

_____

_____

Who said it, and when?

_____

_____

_____

Why was it such a great compliment?

One of the deepest
longings of the human
soul is the longing
to be seen.

— JOHN O'DONOHUE

Every action of our lives
touches on some chord that
will vibrate in eternity.

— EDWIN HUBBELL CHAPIN

YOU ARE SOMEBODY'S ROLE MODEL. MAYBE A FAMILY MEMBER, MAYBE SOMEONE IN YOUR PROFESSION OR HOBBY, MAYBE SOMEONE WHO LOOKS UP TO YOU FOR OTHER REASONS. BUT SOMEONE OUT THERE ADMIRES AND HOPES TO EMULATE YOU IN SOME WAY.

How might you act differently, knowing this?

Think of asking for help as giving someone a wonderful opportunity. People want to help.

WHEN I WAS YOUNG, MY MOTHER TOLD ME THE BEST WAY TO WELCOME A NEW NEIGHBOR WAS NOT TO KNOCK ON THEIR DOOR AND SAY HELLO, BRING FOOD, INVITE THEM TO DINNER, OR OFFER TO HELP THEM UNPACK—THOUGH THOSE ARE ALL NICE THINGS TO DO. THE BEST WAY TO MAKE THEM FEEL WELCOME IS TO ASK THEM TO DO YOU A FAVOR.

THAT ENFOLDS THEM INTO YOUR COMMUNITY RIGHT AWAY.

WHO CAN YOU WELCOME BY ASKING A FAVOR?

I can ask _____ for:

Celebrate something – anything! – today!

HANG A BANNER, BRING FLOWERS, OR OTHERWISE DECORATE TO CELEBRATE:

- Someone's recovery from an illness
- Beginning a challenging task
- The first day of school
- A rainy day
- The end of the week
- The first flower opening in your garden
- The leaves changing in autumn
- A friend's visit

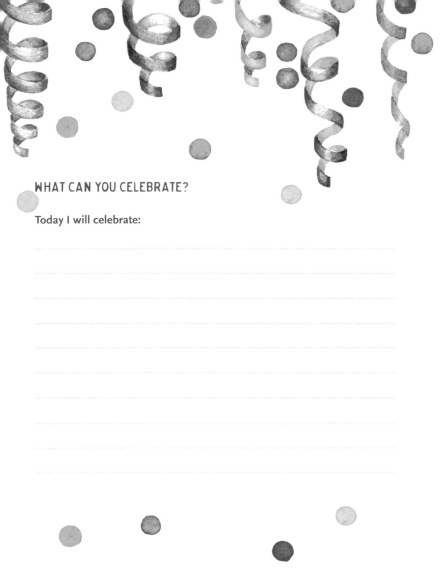

WHAT CAN YOU CELEBRATE?

Today I will celebrate:

PUT ON YOUR OWN OXYGEN MASK FIRST, BEFORE ASSISTING OTHERS.

— EVERY FLIGHT ATTENDANT, EVER

ARE YOU WEARING YOUR OXYGEN MASK?

Is there something essential (sleep? downtime? hydration? affection?) that you're not quite getting enough of to thrive?

....

....

....

Is there anything you can adjust, to get more of this?

....

....

....

IF YOU'RE WEARING YOUR OWN OXYGEN MASK, YOU'LL BE BETTER ABLE TO HELP OTHERS WITH WHAT THEY NEED.

Before I can walk in another's shoes, I must first remove my own.

— AUTHOR UNKNOWN

OUR SHOES PROTECT US, BUT THEY ALSO KEEP US FROM FEELING THE GROUND.

What is limiting your compassion for other people?

What is one thing you could try, to expand your perspective?

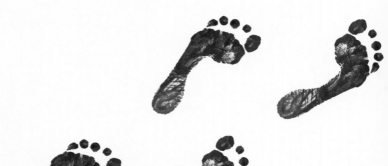

One touch of nature makes
the whole world kin.

— WILLIAM SHAKESPEARE,
TROILUS AND CRESSIDA

INVITE NATURE INTO YOUR LIFE TODAY.

- Spend time listening to the birds
- Put a leafy plant on the windowsill
- Gather pinecones, seashells, pebbles, or acorns and use them as a centerpiece

Other ideas you have:

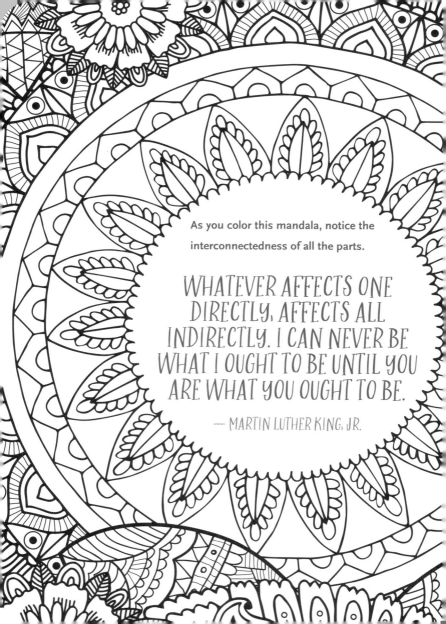

As you color this mandala, notice the interconnectedness of all the parts.

WHATEVER AFFECTS ONE DIRECTLY, AFFECTS ALL INDIRECTLY. I CAN NEVER BE WHAT I OUGHT TO BE UNTIL YOU ARE WHAT YOU OUGHT TO BE.

— MARTIN LUTHER KING, JR.

Create community
where you find it.

TRADITIONAL SUPPORT SYSTEMS ARE CHANGING AS FAMILY AND FRIENDS LIVE FARTHER AWAY, AND WE DON'T ALWAYS CREATE NEW SUPPORT SYSTEMS WITHIN OUR OWN COMMUNITY.

Who in your life do you feel drawn to?

How can you invite them to connect?

If you are more fortunate than others it is better to build a longer table than a taller fence.

— AUTHOR UNKNOWN

Who can you invite to your table?

_____

_____

_____

_____

BE A KINDNESS WARRIOR.

THE WORD "PROTEST" ORIGINALLY COMES FROM A LATIN WORD
MEANING "TO PUBLICLY DECLARE." ADD YOUR VOICE TO A
WORTHY CAUSE.

What's one important cause you believe in?

What actions can you take to support that cause?

. . . IF YOU ARE FREE, YOU NEED TO FREE SOMEBODY ELSE. IF YOU HAVE SOME POWER, THEN YOUR JOB IS TO EMPOWER SOMEBODY ELSE.

— TONI MORRISON

LIFE IS FULL OF TIMES YOU WISH YOU HAD A "DO-OVER."

Recall a time when you were less than kind. Write about it here. What happened?

Now write about what you wish you had done differently.

YOU CAN'T CHANGE WHAT HAPPENED. SOMETIMES AN APOLOGY HELPS; SOMETIMES IT DOESN'T. ALL YOU CAN DO IS MAKE DIFFERENT CHOICES IN THE FUTURE. BE KIND TO YOURSELF, TRY TO LET GO OF GUILT, AND INSTEAD FOCUS ON WHAT YOU'LL CHOOSE TO DO NEXT TIME.

Give something your full attention.

PRACTICE BEING PRESENT BY FOCUSING FULLY ON A
TASK TODAY. DO JUST THAT ONE THING. NOTICE YOUR
FIVE SENSES AS YOU WASH DISHES, DRIVE TO WORK,
OR WAIT IN LINE.

What did you focus on?

How did it feel, during and after?

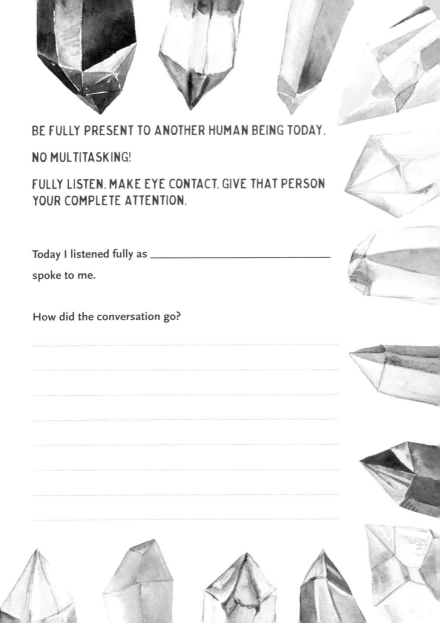

BE FULLY PRESENT TO ANOTHER HUMAN BEING TODAY.

NO MULTITASKING!

FULLY LISTEN. MAKE EYE CONTACT. GIVE THAT PERSON YOUR COMPLETE ATTENTION.

Today I listened fully as _____

spoke to me.

How did the conversation go?

_____

_____

_____

_____

_____

_____

_____

_____

FRIENDSHIP MULTIPLIES JOYS, AND DIVIDES GRIEFS.

— FRANCIS BACON

SPEND TIME WITH YOUR FRIENDS. IT'S GOOD FOR YOUR (EMOTIONAL!) HEALTH.

What friends would you like to see sometime soon?

_____

_____

_____

What might you do with each of them, and when?

_____

_____

_____

_____

Give them a call, email, or text!

Emotional Bravery

THE ONLY WAY TO BE GENUINELY CLOSE TO OTHER PEOPLE IS TO OPEN YOUR HEART TO THEM. START GRADUALLY TODAY: MOVE BEYOND THE WEATHER TO SHARE A CONCERN YOU HAVE (FAMILY, A MINOR PROBLEM, A WORRY, A SADNESS). MAKE SPACE IN THE CONVERSATION FOR THE OTHER PERSON TO SHARE AS WELL.

Vulnerability is . . . the birthplace of joy, of creativity, of belonging, of love.

— BRENÉ BROWN

Today I went a little deeper in conversation with

_____ .

What did you share?

What did they say? Did they share anything in return? (Don't write down anything that was told to you in confidence.)

How did you feel afterward?

Kindness begins at home.

BUILD YOUR IDEAL EMOTIONAL HOME. WRITE OR DRAW IN THE ROOMS:

love

KINDNESS

distance

remorse

trust

generosity

patience

joy

What is the foundation made of?

What traits live in your home, in common rooms and more private second-story rooms?

What is put away in the attic?

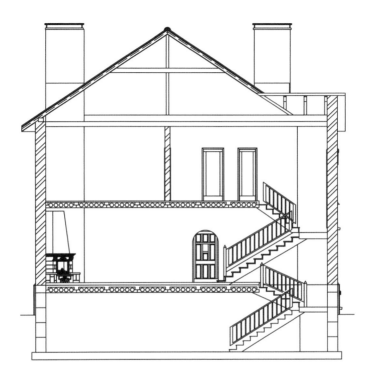

What in your home feels welcoming or cozy?

_____

_____

What is in need of repair and strengthening?

_____

_____

APPRECIATION IS TO HUMANS WHAT THE SUN IS FOR PLANTS.

— FRANK IVERSEN

Whom do you appreciate, and what do you appreciate about them?

Pick one person to express appreciation to. How can you show it?

Try to be a rainbow in someone's cloud.

— MAYA ANGELOU

MARY MCGLONE is a writer, teacher, and devoted journaler. She currently works as a college writing consultant and professor of literature and writing, frequently using journaling and poetry to awaken students' honesty and connection to words. Mary previously taught English at the secondary level and developed an award-winning writing center at a Long Island, New York high school. She is also the author of a book about genealogy inspired by her family history.

Mary practices kindness toward people and other living creatures at every opportunity. Among her superpowers are unscrewing jars with her feet and writing this book while in a wrist cast.